Contents

A Note to Parents

Elmo and his friends on Sesame Street love to explore and learn about the world around them. *Simple Science Experiments with Elmo and Friends* shows children how to do the same thing right in their own homes and neighborhoods. In this book, you'll find exciting experiments that introduce kids to science and help them develop skills that are key to scientific learning and inquiry: *observation, investigation, reporting,* and *reflecting* on the "big idea." The experiments work on multiple educational levels, so they are fun and easy for children as young as 3 and as old as 7.

The book is divided into two parts: experiments that make use of the element *water,* and experiments that involve *earth* (a word that kids will learn describes both our planet *and* dirt or soil.) The only materials you'll need are simple things that can be found around the house or outside in a backyard or park. Some experiments are best done with a grown-up's help—especially for the younger children—but most are easy and safe for kids to undertake on their own. In addition to the experiments, you'll find 9 engaging activity spreads designed to reinforce scientific concepts presented in the projects. The activities include *connect-the-dots, matching,* and *search-and-find* puzzles that both entertain and educate.

To get the most out of this book, set aside some time to perform the experiments with your child. Before you begin each project, ask your child if he or she can predict what will happen. When you finish, talk about what he or she observed and reflect on what happened. Be sure to keep an eye out for several special boxes that appear throughout the book that amplify information related to the experiments or highlight important science vocabulary words.

Finally, look at the pages labeled "Science Journal" at the back of this book. Help your child record his or her observations, either in words or in pictures. All of these processes offer unique educational experiences for your child as well as shared learning opportunities for you and your child together.

Super Grover 2.0

Keep an eye out for Super Grover 2.0, Sesame Street's biggest science fan. He pops up here and there to encourage children to observe, ask questions, and reflect on the scientific concepts covered in the experiments.

Murray's Science Words on the Street

Murray loves new words, so look for his special "Science Words on the Street" box, which highlights important scientific vocabulary words and offers easy-to-understand definitions.

Extra Caution

Sometimes you will see this caution symbol. It indicates that a project requires extra care, and possibly supervision from an adult.

Science Journal

Several pages entitled "Science Journal" are provided at the back of the book to encourage kids to create a real "Science Journal" by drawing a picture of what he or she notices in each experiment or by writing down words or phrases that describe what he or she learned while performing the experiment.

Happy Scientists

Did you know that anyone can be a scientist? All you have to do is **observe, investigate, report,** and **reflect** on what you've learned. So join Elmo and his friends as they have fun exploring water and earth using science!

Murray's Science Words on the Street

observe
To use your senses—sight, sound, smell, touch, and taste—to find out more about something.

investigate
To do things that will help you find the answer to your question.

report
To tell someone about what you have learned, either by talking about it or writing it down.

reflect
To think about what has been learned, ask more questions, and identify the "big idea."

Did you know the word "earth" has many meanings? It means "soil" or "dirt." We plant seeds in the earth. But it is also the name of the planet we live on—the planet Earth!

Why are water and earth so important? Because they help all living things stay alive!

Plants and animals can't live long without water. And earth—which in this case means "soil" or "dirt"—contains food that helps living things grow.

Draw a circle around all the tools that help Elmo and his friends **observe, investigate, report,** and **reflect** on what they see around them.

Count how many tools they are using.

Write down the number of scientific tools they find.

Answer

Part 1:

Water Experiments

Water Experiments

Water covers most of our planet Earth. This is very important because animals, plants, people, and fish like Elmo's friend Dorothy need water to live. Did you know that people's bodies are made up mostly of water? That is right! About 75% of you is water! Scientists study water because it is so important to life. There are so many fun things to learn about water.

Liquid, Solid, Gas

I love to splish-splash in the water in my birdbath! But did you know that water is not just a **liquid?** It comes in different forms depending on how hot or cold the air is around it. It's easy to change water into its different forms. Try it yourself!

What you need:
- Water
- A paper cup
- An ice cube tray
- A teakettle

Let's Observe!

Water freezes at 32 degrees Fahrenheit and boils at 212 degrees Fahrenheit. Wow! **32 degrees is super cold. 212 degrees is super hot!**

What to do:

Caution! Hot water and steam

1. Fill the paper cup with water and pour it into an ice cube tray.

2. Place the tray in a freezer for a few hours.

3. Take the tray out, and observe what happened to the water. What do you notice? How does it feel? Is it cold or hot? Is it wet or dry? Is it soft or hard? The **liquid** water has turned into **solid** ice cubes.

4. Next, put the ice cube tray on a counter and wait a few hours. What happened to the water? Is the water still hard? Did the ice melt back into a liquid?

5. Carefully pour the water back into your cup.

6. Last, pour the water from the cup into a teakettle and make sure a grown-up heats it up for you.

7. Watch from a distance as it boils. The cloudy mist that comes out of the spout is steam, which is a **gas**.

liquid	solid	gas
Something that flows smoothly and takes the shape of any container, like water.	Matter that has a definite shape and always takes up the same amount of space.	Matter that has no definite size or shape; it is air-like and expands freely to fill any space available, no matter how much of it there is.

Murray's Science Words on the Street

Float or Sink?

I really, really want to teach my pet rock Rocco to swim. But every time I put him in water he just sinks! I'm starting to think some things float better than others depending on what they're made of. I've asked Elmo and my friends to help me **predict** which things will float and which will sink. Can you help me, too? Let's investigate!

What you need:

- Some safe objects from around the house like a metal spoon, a building block, a ball of rubber bands, a bar of soap, an eraser, a toy ball or boat, or a piece of fruit
- A large bowl (or the kitchen/bathroom sink) filled with water
- Your *Science Journal* or a notebook
- A crayon

Let's Observe!

Time to unleash the power of investigation! Look at your journal and pick out one thing that sank and one that floated. What do you predict will happen if you used a rubber band to put them together? Do they still float? Do they still sink?
Try it and let's observe what happens!

What to do:

1. Collect the objects and draw a picture of each one in your *Science Journal* or in a notebook.

2. Form a **hypothesis** about which ones will sink or float and give your reasons why.

3. Fill a large bowl or sink with water and experiment by placing each object, one at a time, into the water. Which objects floated? Which ones sank? Was your hypothesis correct? Were you surprised when something you thought would float, sank?

4. Look at your notebook and circle all the objects that floated. Count how many floated.

Murray's Science Words on the Street

predict

To use a little bit of information to guess what will happen next.

hypothesis

An idea about what could happen and why.

Which One's Colder?

Hello! Super Grover 2.0 here, ready to use my super sense of touch to figure out which gets colder faster—water or air?

I predict that water will get colder faster because heat leaves water more **rapidly** than it leaves air. I have asked my friends to assist me in this very interesting experiment. Let us all try it together.

What you need:

- Water
- Two paper or plastic cups (with lids to prevent spills, if you have them)
- A timer or clock
- Your *Science Journal* or a notebook

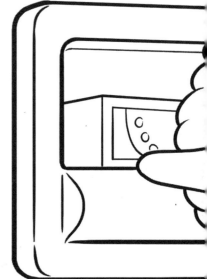

What to do:

1. Fill one cup with water and leave the other one empty.

2. Place both cups in the freezer, and set the timer for ten minutes.

3. When ten minutes have passed, take the cups out of the freezer and, with your eyes closed, feel the cups.

4. Which one is colder? The one full of water, or the one with only air inside?

5. Ask a grown-up to help you write down what you learned in your *Science Journal* or in a notebook.

rapidly
Quickly, fast.

Murray's Science
Word on the Street

17

Amazing Water Maze

Water travels a very long way before it enters your home. It forms in rain clouds then falls from the sky into reservoirs. Reservoirs are man-made lakes where water is collected for use by people in nearby cities and towns. From there, water flows through pipes and through a faucet and into your sink, tub, or shower.

Use your finger or a crayon to trace the water from the rain cloud to the cup in Elmo's hand.

START

18

FINISH

19

Drinking Flowers

Plants drink water to live, just like people do. But plants don't have mouths or beaks; they soak up water through tiny tubes called **capillaries**. Water moves up through the stem and through the whole plant, even the petals! Let's observe how plants drink! What do you notice?

What you need:
- **Three bottles filled with water**
- **Three different food colorings, such as red, blue, and yellow**
- **Three white flowers (carnations work well)**
- **Safety scissors**

PARTS OF A FLOWER

PISTIL   PETAL

SEPAL

STEM   STAMEN

LEAF

What to do:

1. Fill the bottles with water

2. Add two or three drops of a food coloring to each. Use a different color in each bottle.

3. Trim the stems of the three white flowers on a **diagonal**. This makes a bigger hole for the water to flow through.

4. Put one flower in each bottle and let them sit overnight.

5. Observe the flowers in the morning. The petals will have turned the color of the water they are drinking!

RED

BLUE

YELLOW

Murray's Science
Words on the Street

capillaries
Tiny, hair-like, branching tubes.

diagonal
A slanted line.

Gummy Science

Me love gummy candies almost as much as cookies. Every gummy is yummy, which rhymes. Gummies are also chewy because they are made of sugar and sticky, gooey stuff called starch and gelatin. If me put gummy candy in water and wait until morning, something amazing happens: it grows!

How can this happen? Me learned that starch and gelatin do not easily **dissolve** (or fall apart) in water. But starch and gelatin **absorb** water, or soak it up like a sponge. As a delicious gummy candy absorbs water, it grows bigger! Try it yourself and observe what happens!

What you need:

- **Gummy candies**
- **Ruler**
- **Your *Science Journal* or a notebook**
- **Crayon**
- **Plastic container filled with water**
- **A paper towel**

Let's Observe!

Stand clear! Creating a giant gummy bear is a job for a super hero like me! What do you think will happen if I leave the gummy bear in water one more day? Will it keep growing? Time to find out by unleashing the power of observation!

22

What to do:

1. Pick your favorite gummy candy—bears, worms, anything will do!

2. Measure the candy's length and width, or trace around it. You or a grown-up can record the measurements on your *Science Journal* pages or in a notebook.

3. Put the gummy candy in a container of water. Wait 24 hours, then carefully remove the gummy and place it on a paper towel.

4. Measure it again and **compare** the difference in size. What do you notice? Is it bigger or smaller? How much did it grow?

5. Record your findings in your *Science Journal* or notebook.

Murray's Science Words on the Street

dissolve
When a solid is mixed with a liquid, and the solid breaks down into pieces so small they can't be seen in the liquid.

absorb
To take in or soak in (as with water).

compare
To figure out if things are the same or different.

23

Ice Melting Race

It's a warm, sunny day and Bert predicts that if he puts an ice cube on black paper, it will melt faster than an ice cube Ernie puts on white paper. But Ernie predicts his ice cube will melt first. To figure out whose ice cube will melt faster, they have an ice cube "race."

Whose ice cube do you think will melt faster? Bert's ice cube on black paper, or Ernie's ice cube on white paper? Who do you predict will be the winner?

Bert wins the ice cube race! Why? The ice on Bert's black paper melted first because the darker paper absorbs heat, and the light white paper **reflects** it. Now you try!

What you need:

- A sheet of white construction paper
- A sheet of black construction paper
- Ice cubes
- Your *Science Journal* or a notebook

Let's Observe!

I shall unleash my super powers of observation. Do dark colored clothes keep you warmer? Yes! Black or dark colored clothes absorb heat so they are warmer, especially when worn in the sun.

What to do:

1. Wait for a sunny day and lay one sheet of white construction paper and one sheet of black construction paper on a dry, flat surface outside.

2. Put one ice cube on each piece of paper. Ready, set, go!

3. Observe which ice cube melts faster in the sun. You can even use a timer to find out how long it takes for each to melt. Which one melts faster? **Compare** the two cubes. What do they look like?

4. Report your results to a grown-up and ask them to help you write them down in your *Science Journal* or in a notebook so you can look them over when you're done and draw a **conclusion**.

And they're off!

reflect
To bounce off of.

compare
To figure out if two or more things are the same or different.

conclusion
To summarize your findings after doing an investigation.

Murray's Science
Words on the Street

Ocean in a Bottle

Cookie wants to sail the high seas, but he doesn't have a boat. So, he's going to make a pretend ocean in a bottle. Cookie heard he can do this by mixing water and oil. But no matter how hard he shakes, oil and water simply won't mix! Why? Water is heavier, or **denser**, than oil. The heavier water sinks to the bottom and the lighter oil rises to the top.

Oil and water might not be good for mixing, but they are great for making a pretend ocean! Cookie adds a little blue food coloring, some glitter, and shells to the water to make it look like a real ocean! You try it, too. Set sail and observe what happens!

What you need:
- A large, clear plastic bottle with a cap
- Blue food coloring
- Shells and glitter (if you want)
- A funnel
- Vegetable oil

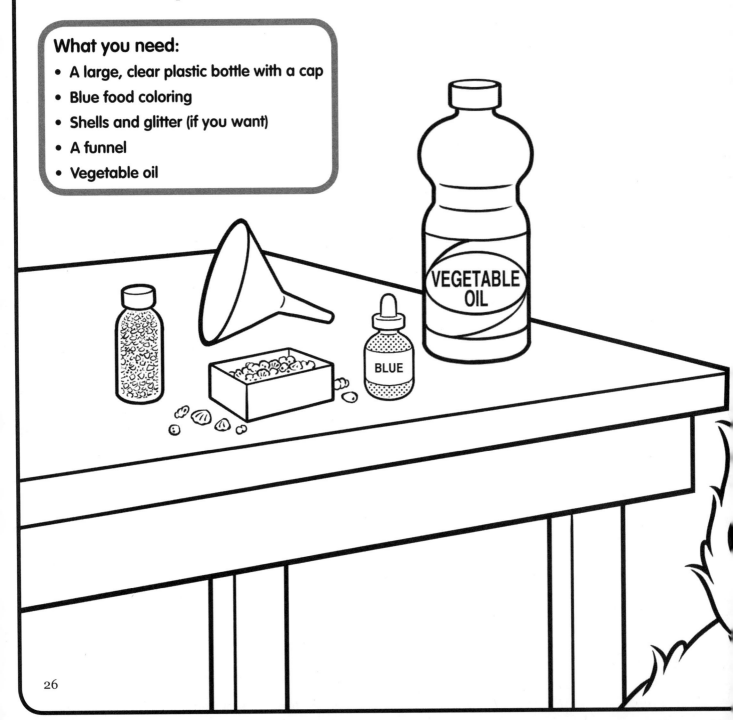

What to do:

1. Fill the bottle ¾ full of water.

2. Add blue food coloring to make your ocean.

3. Add shells and glitter to make your ocean look even more like the real thing.

4. Place a funnel over the opening of the bottle, and add the oil.

5. Screw the cap on tightly and shake the bottle.

6. Observe that the oil and water mix for a second then separate back into "ocean" and "sky."

7. Turn the bottle on its side. Rock it back and forth and you have ocean waves in a bottle!

dense
Tightly packed together, heavy.

Murray's Science
Word on the Street

27

Find the Amphibian

I love **amphibians**. They are creatures that are as gooey, wet, slippery, and slimy as Slimey! But amphibians are different than Slimey. They live only in the water when they are babies, breathe air as adults, have four legs, and go through **metamorphosis**. Connect the dots to reveal three amphibians! Name each amphibian.

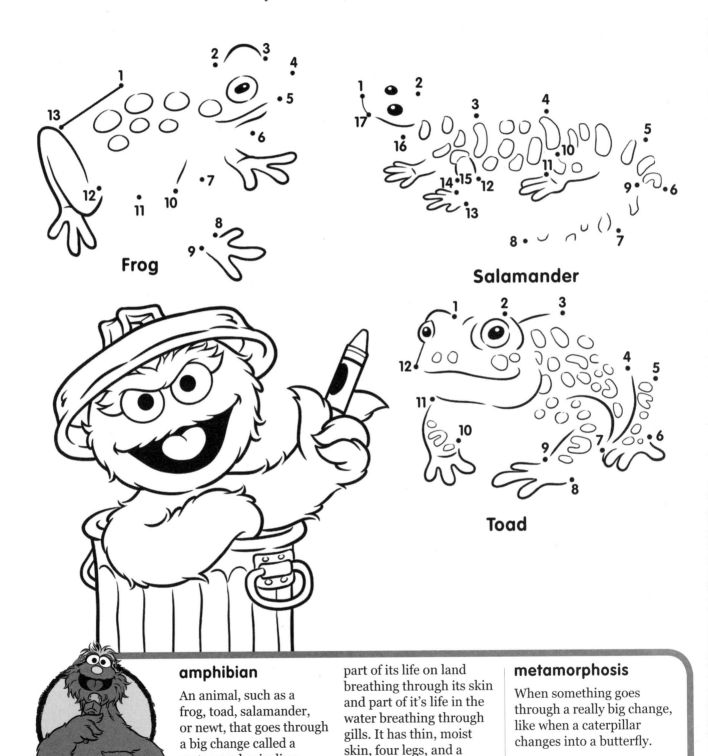

Frog

Salamander

Toad

amphibian

An animal, such as a frog, toad, salamander, or newt, that goes through a big change called a metamorphosis; lives part of its life on land breathing through its skin and part of it's life in the water breathing through gills. It has thin, moist skin, four legs, and a backbone.

metamorphosis

When something goes through a really big change, like when a caterpillar changes into a butterfly.

Look at all the **tadpoles**. Tadpoles are amphibians also, because they are baby frogs.
Help Elmo and Abby count the tadpoles in the tank. How many did you count?

Answer

Blowing Bubbles

It's BubbleFest on Sesame Street! Elmo has asked his good friend Abby Cadabby to help him make bubbles! Together they mix up a **formula** made of soap, water, and sugar. When they are done they can blow bubbles. So join them and mix up a batch of bubble formula yourself!

What you need:

- ½ cup of dishwashing liquid
- 2 cups of water
- 2 teaspoons of sugar
- A dab of food coloring (if you want)
- A shallow pan
- A bubble wand (store bought or made with pipe cleaners)

Did you use magic to make these bubbles?

Let's Observe!

Stand Clear! I am a superhero who likes to **engineer** new designs! Make bubble wands in different shapes—round, square, rectangular—using pipe cleaners. What happens when you make bubbles with these wands? Are they bigger? Smaller? Round? Square?

What to do:

1. Measure all of your **ingredients** (dishwashing liquid, water, sugar, and food coloring) for your **formula**. Pour them into a shallow pan, and mix well.

2. Dip your bubble wand in the mixture, and blow through it gently.

3. Count how many bubbles you can make!

ingredient
One of the things that makes up a recipe or formula.

formula
Instructions that tell you how much of each ingredient should be mixed together to make something else.

engineer
To design or build something for a certain purpose or to solve a problem.

Murray's Science
Words on the Street

31

A Sticky Situation

Honey is one of Baby Bear's favorite foods because it is so sweet and **sticky.** But would you ever guess that water is sticky, too? It isn't exactly sticky the way honey is—it won't make your fingers gooey. But water does stick to itself! In science, when something sticks to itself it is called **cohesion.**

What might happen if two streams of water run very close together? Let's investigate!

What you need:
- A sharp pencil
- A Styrofoam cup
- Water

The next time you are in a foamy, soapy bubble bath, try unleashing your powers of observation and notice how the bubbles stick to each other. That's **cohesion.** Reflect on that!

What to do:

1. Ask a grown up to use the pencil to poke two little holes in the bottom of the Styrofoam cup (the holes should be very close together so that they almost touch).

2. Hold the cup over a sink.

3. Pour the water into the cup.

4. As the water comes out of each hole, quickly pinch the two streams together to form one stream.

5. If it doesn't work the first time, don't give up! It can take a few tries to get it right.

6. What do you notice?

Caution!
Sharp pencil

Look! The water sticks to itself!

Murray's Science Words on the Street

sticky

When something hangs on to something else without clips or other help.

cohesion

When something sticks to itself.

Indoor Rainstorm

I love dancing in the rain. So does Elmo. But when it rains hard outside, we have to stay inside. So, Elmo and I wondered if we could make it rain inside while it is raining outside! Let's see if we can do it!

A grown-up needs to help you make your indoor rainstorm. Ask the grown-up to boil water in a teakettle and then hold a bowl of ice water above the boiling kettle. What do you observe?

Swirly steam! (Stay far away from the steam because it is really hot!

When steam touches an icy-cold bowl, it cools down. Then the steam turns back into tiny drops that **cling** to the bowl. Scientists call this **condensation**. As the drops get bigger and heavier, they fall... Splat! Just like real raindrops.

What you need:
- **Water**
- **A teakettle**
- **A bowl**
- **Ice**
- **A grown-up**

Let's Observe!

Observe what happens when you sip a super cold drink on a super hot day. Water drops form and slide down the side! That is **condensation,** and it is super amazing!

34

What to do:

1. Add water to the teakettle and to the bowl.

2. Ask a grown-up boil the water for you.

3. Add ice to the water in the bowl.

4. Ask the grown-up to hold the bowl of ice water high above the teakettle.

5. Stand away from the hot steam and watch the indoor rainstorm!

6. Draw a picture of what you see in your *Science Journal* or in a notebook.

Murray's Science Words on the Street

cling
To stick to, hang on to.

condensation
When steam cools quickly and turns into water drops.

Rainbow in a Jar

Rainbows are so magical! I love to swoop and fly around them after a rainstorm. A teacher fairy once told me how a rainbow is made. After it rains, sunlight shines through little drops of water that stay **suspended** in the air. The drops act like a **prism,** which breaks up light into many beautiful colors. Rainbows are so amazing that I like to make them at home. Or help Rosita color in the rainbow from her window. Do you want to make a rainbow with me?

Let's Observe!

Behold! When light passes through water, it breaks up into a rainbow made up of seven different colors: red, orange, yellow, green, blue, indigo, and violet. It is hard to imagine, but did you know there are even more colors in a rainbow, but they are invisible!

What to do:

1. Fill the jar with water and set it on the windowsill in bright sunlight.

2. Place a sheet of white paper on the floor in front of the window. What happened? Did a rainbow form on the paper?

3. What colors do you see? Think of the name "Roy G. Biv" to help you remember the colors in a rainbow: red, orange, yellow, green, blue, indigo, violet.

4. Use your crayons to trace and color in the rainbow.

What you need:

- A glass jar filled with water
- A windowsill
- A sunny day
- A sheet of white paper
- Crayons

Murray's Science Words on the Street

suspend
To hang.

prism
Something clear, often with slanted sides, that breaks light up into many colors.

37

Puddle Jumping

Rain helps beautiful flowers grow and fills our reservoirs with the water we drink. Rain also keeps streets clean, freshens the air, and makes puddles, which are really fun for splashing in. See if you can spot 10 differences between these two pictures of a rainy day on Sesame Street.

39

Have a Ball... or Two

Hi, Super Grover 2.0 here to unleash the power of observation! Let's see what happens when we spin two different kinds of balls in bowls of water. The first kind of ball is a fuzzy tennis ball. The second is a **smooth** rubber ball. Stand clear!

Okay, here we go. I am spinning both types of balls in water and... Hm.

The fuzzy tennis ball does not spin as fast as the smooth tennis ball. I wonder what is the problem? I know. When any two things rub against each other, they kind of grab each other. When this happens it is called **friction**. Friction slows things down. The fuzzy ball spins slower then the smooth ball because the "fuzz" creates more friction with the water!

Fuzzy Tennis Ball

Smooth Rubber Ball

What you need:
- Two big bowls
- Water
- A rubber ball
- A tennis ball

40

What to do:

1. Fill the bowls halfway with water.

2. Put the fuzzy tennis ball into the first bowl of water and spin it. Observe what happens. Does it spin fast or slow?

3. Put the smooth rubber ball in the second bowl of water and spin it. Observe what happens. Does it spin fast or slow?

4. Try spinning both balls in the water at the same time. Observe which ball spins faster.

5. If you can, try spinning other kinds of balls in water—a Ping-Pong ball, a ball of clay, a popcorn ball! What happens? Which balls spin fast? Which balls spin slow?

6. Tell a grown-up what you observed and ask him or her to write it down for you in your *Science Journal* or notebook.

Murray's Science Words on the Street

smooth
Having nothing that sticks out or caves in. Even.

friction
When one thing rubs against another.

Pepper Magic

I am performing a magic trick for my buddy, Bert. I sprinkle pepper into a bowl of water, then dip my finger into the bowl and Pffft! The pepper rushes away from my finger! Bert wants to know how I did it? I want him to think it's magic, but I will let you in on my secret.

Remember in "Sticky Situation" on page 32, we learned that water sticks to itself? Well, water is most sticky at the top, or **surface,** where it **contacts** the air. Scientists call this **surface tension.**

Water is so good at sticking to itself at the surface that it forms a kind of skin. Look at a glass of water from the side and observe closely. What do you see? It looks like there is a clear skin on top!

Soap makes water less sticky. To perform my cool trick for Bert, I secretly rubbed soap all over my finger before I started. When I dipped my soapy finger into the bowl, the water at the surface stopped sticking together and spread apart and the pepper spread out with it. It looked like magic, but it wasn't! It was science!

What you need:

- A bowl
- Water
- Dishwashing liquid
- A teaspoon of black pepper

How did you do that?!

What to do:

1. Fill a bowl with water.

2. Rub dishwashing liquid onto your finger (secretly, before you do the trick).

3. Sprinkle black pepper into the middle of the water.

4. Dip your soapy finger into the center of the peppery water.

5. Watch the pepper move away from your finger.

Presto!

SOAP

Murray's Science
Words on the Street

surface	contact	surface tension
The top layer of something.	To touch.	When water at the surface sticks to itself and forms a kind of skin.

43

Wiggly Worms

Worms are so wonderfully yucky! I love worms—especially my pal, Slimey. It's fun to make "pretend" worms that are so yucky they almost look real. I made them out of little pieces of cooked spaghetti that I added to water mixed with vinegar and baking soda.

In science, when you mix things together, sometimes something new happens. In this case, everything starts to gurgle and fizz and bubbles form. When the bubbles burst, the "worms" wiggle. Pretty yucky, huh? Try it out yourself and observe what happens!

What you need:

- A big bowl
- 1 cup of water
- 1 cup of white vinegar
- 2 tablespoons of baking soda
- Cooked spaghetti broken into worm-sized pieces

What to do:

1. Add water and vinegar to the bowl and mix.

2. Add the baking soda.

3. Add the spaghetti pieces.

4. Watch the pretend worms wiggle!

Every Drop Counts

There is a lot of water on our planet, but did you know that only a very small amount of it is drinkable? Most of our water can be found in oceans, but it is way too salty to drink. There's plenty of fresh water high in the mountains, but it is frozen and hard to reach. That's why it's important for all of us to save water.

We want to be sure there is enough water for everyone, right?

Can you spot the water wasters on Sesame Street? Circle the ones you find. How many water wasters do you see?

Write the number in the box.

WATER WASTERS

Drinkable Water

Land

Water

47

Part 2:

Earth Experiments

Earth Experiments

Did you know that the word "earth" has two meanings? "Earth" is the name of our planet, *and* the word "earth" can also mean soil (or dirt). In this part of the book, you'll find experiments about soil and the things you find in it (like rocks, plants, and insects). You'll also see experiments about our planet and how big things like wind and gravity affect it. So head outside to your backyard or to a local park. They are perfect places for studying earth, the soil, and Earth, our planet.

Hitting Pay Dirt

Dirt or soil, whatever you call that grungy stuff, I love it! Did you know dirt has things like tiny rocks, **humus,** and sandy **particles** in it? I like to observe it closely. First, I mix dirt with water, then I shake it up and let it settle into layers called **sediment.** The heaviest stuff sinks to the bottom and the lightest stuff rests on top. A magnifying glass helps me observe each layer closely. I like to compare how the layers are the same and different. Try it yourself. You'll think dirt is as wonderfully yucky as I do!

What you need:

- A large jar with a lid that can be screwed shut
- A cup of soil
- Water
- A magnifying glass
- Crayons
- Paper

Let's Observe!

Observe, question, and investigate! To make this experiment even more super, collect dirt from different places: a garden, a park, or a relative's yard. Use a magnifying glass to examine the different soils you found. Using your senses, look for three ways they are the same, and three ways they are different.

What to do:

1. Scoop the soil into the jar.

2. Add water until the jar is ¾ full.

3. Tighten the lid.

4. Shake hard for a few seconds.

5. Wait two hours until the soil settles.

6. Using a magnifying glass, observe each layer closely.

7. Draw a picture of what you see in your *Science Journal* or a notebook.

Murray's Science Words on the Street

humus

Dark material in soil that is made up of rotting plants and other things that were once alive.

particle

A tiny piece of something, like dust.

sediment

Matter that settles to the bottom of a liquid.

Rock On

My pal Bert loves to sort things. He's just like a scientist that way! Scientists put things in order by **sorting** and **classifying** them. Then they study objects by comparing one thing to another. Scientists who study rocks are called **geologists**. Bert and our friends are collecting, sorting, comparing, and classifying rocks from the park. Want to try it with us? Pretend you're a geologist and collect rocks from your backyard or a nearby park or beach. Then sort and classify them by size, shape, and color. Being a scientist is so much fun!

What you need:

- A pail or sturdy box for collecting your rocks
- Ten big rocks, rinsed clean. (These should be at least as big as your palm)
- Pages from your *Science Journal* or notebook, and crayons

Let's Observe!

Here's a super fact. The most common rock on Earth is called **basalt.** It comes from volcanoes!

What to do:

1. Collect ten rocks that are different sizes, shapes, and colors.

2. Use your senses to look at the rocks, then sort and classify them by size. Place them into two piles—big rocks and small rocks.

3. Mix up the rocks, then sort and classify them by color: light rocks and dark rocks; or red rocks and gray rocks.

4. Mix them up again, and sort and classify by shape: lumpy rocks and smooth rocks. Count out loud as you point to each.

5. Can you think of another way to sort and classify rocks? Sparkly and dull? Flat and round? Think up your own!

6. With your crayons, draw pictures of your rocks in your *Science Journal* or notebook.

Murray's Science Words on the Street

sort

To group or separate objects based on how they are alike and different.

classify

To identify what makes things alike.

geologist

A scientist who studies rocks.

Backyard Mountains

Elmo loves building sandcastles at the beach. Elmo giggles when big crashy waves make Elmo's sandcastle fall apart. When water makes something fall apart it is called **erosion**. Water can even make big things like **boulders** and mountains fall apart. It just takes a long, long time. Elmo and his friends are going to learn about erosion by building three mini-mountains right here on Sesame Street. Give it a try and observe what happens!

What you need:

- Enough rocks, sand, and dirt to make three mini-mountains out of each
- Water
- A plastic cup
- Pages from your *Science Journal* or notebook, and crayons

Hey!

Let's Observe! It is I, Super Grover 2.0! Did you know that the Grand Canyon, which is super-big, was formed by erosion from wind, water, and ice? Erosion in the Grand Canyon took millions of years! That is a very, very long time!

What to do:

1. In your yard or a local park, build three mini-mountains: one out of rocks, one out of sand, and one out of dirt.

2. First, pour a cup of water over the sand mountain. Predict what will happen? Did it erode the sand a lot or a little?

3. Next, pour a cup of water over the dirt. Did the water erode the dirt mountain a lot or a little? More or less than the sand?

4. Pour a cup of water over the rocks. Did the rock mountain erode a lot or a little? Did it erode at all? More or less than the sand and dirt?

5. In your *Science Journal* or notebook, draw a picture of your three mountains after you have poured water on them. Put a check next to the mountain that eroded the most.

Murray's Science Words on the Street

erosion

When something (like water or wind) wears away another thing (like a mountain).

boulder

A very large rock.

Buried Treasure

Most people think soil is just a bunch of dirt. But when I look at soil, I see buried treasure! If you look closely, dirt has all kinds of fantastically yucky things hidden in it. Find and circle the hidden treasures on my map.

59

Breathing Trees

Did you ever stand close to a mirror and breath on it? Try it now and then unleash your power of observation! What do you see? The mirror **fogs** up with teeny, tiny water **droplets** from your breath. Did you know trees and plants breathe, too?! They don't have lungs like people do, but they also let off tiny drops of water. I shall now tie a small plastic sandwich bag around a **clump** of leaves and leave it there overnight. In the morning I shall investigate to find out what happens!

Behold! There are tiny drops of water on the inside of the plastic bag. Amazing! Investigating is all in a day's work for Super Grover 2.0!

What you need:

- A small plastic sandwich bag (You'll need a grown-up to help you!)
- A rubber band
- A plant or a tree with a low branch
- Pages from your *Science Journal* or notebook

What to do:

1. Cover a clump of leaves with the plastic bag. (Ask a grown-up to help you.)

2. Wrap a rubber band around the bag and leaves, but not so tight that you break the leaves or stem.

3. Leave the bag on the leaves overnight.

4. Observe what you see. What does it look like? Look at the "fog" under a magnifying glass. What does it look like?

5. Write three words (or ask a grown-up to write them) in your *Science Journal* or notebook to describe what you see. Is it wet? Is it misty?

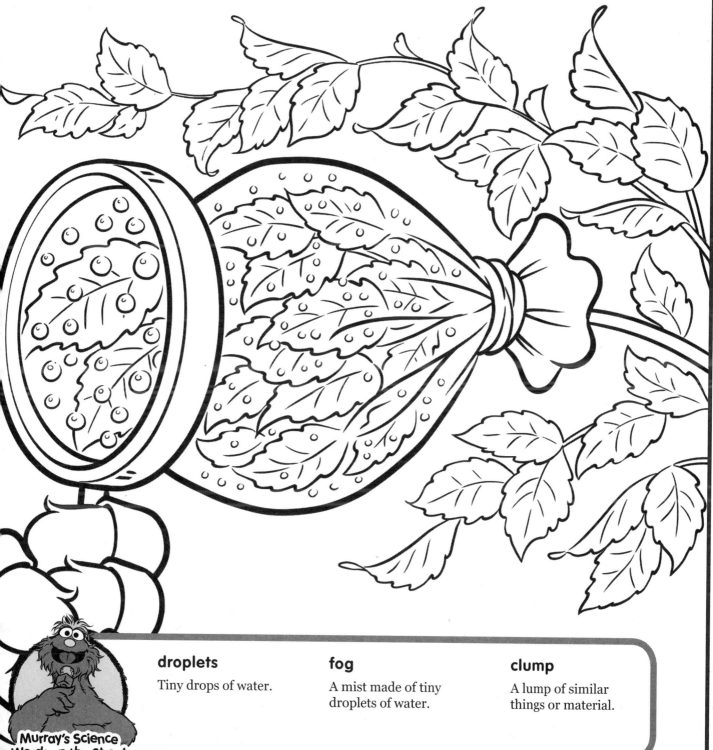

droplets
Tiny drops of water.

fog
A mist made of tiny droplets of water.

clump
A lump of similar things or material.

Murray's Science
Words on the Street

Barking Trees

I'm here in a park with Bert and some of our good friends. Elmo has noticed that bark on some kinds of trees is very different from bark on other kinds of trees. Some trees have smooth bark. Other trees have lumpy, rough bark. Some trees have thick bark; some have thin, papery bark. Scientists look closely at bark and feel it in order to compare and **identify** trees. We're going to **record** how the bark from these trees looks and feels so that we can see how they are the same and different. Try it yourself!

What you need:

- Tracing paper
- Different colored crayons with the paper removed
- Pages from your *Science Journal* or notebook

Let's Observe!

The giant sequoia is the tallest, most super tree there is. Sequoias grow as tall as 380 feet! That's as high as a very tall building. Nearly as high as Super Grover 2.0 can fly! Sequoias also have super bark that is up to three feet thick!

62

What to do:

1. Look for trees with different kinds of bark. How many can you find?

2. Using your senses, see if you can find a tree with dark brown or black bark. Can you find a tree with light gray bark? White bark? How does the bark on each tree feel when you touch it?

3. Use one hand to hold the tracing paper against the tree, and with and the other hand rub the side of a crayon against the paper. Repeat with a few different trees, using different-colored crayons.

4. Look at the trees. Are they big trees or small trees? What do their leaves look like?

5. When you get home, compare your rubbings. How are the tree barks the same? How are they different? Tape or paste your tree rubbings into your *Science Journal* or notebook. Draw a picture of your favorite tree.

Murray's Science Words on the Street

identify
To say or label what something is.

record
To draw a picture or write down what you see.

Counting Tree Rings

The forest is a fantastic place because there are so many fabulous trees to count! You can tell the age of a tree by counting the number of rings on its stump. For example, this tree was 20 years old when it fell down. Count the rings on all the other tree stumps to find their age! Mark the number in the box next to each stump.

Table Top Volcano!

Volcanoes are mountains that have lava, rock **fragments,** and steam flowing out of them. These materials come from deep below the earth's **crust.** Volcanoes throw off sparks that shoot way up into the sky. It's a red-hot light show! *Increíble!* Elmo and I are creating our own make-believe volcano at home. You can make one yourself, but be sure to get a grown-up to help you. Let's give it a try!

What you need:

For your volcano

- 2 cups of salt
- 6 cups of flour
- 4 tablespoons of cooking oil
- 2 cups of water
- A large bowl

For your eruption

- A plastic bottle
- Warm water
- Red food coloring
- Dishwashing liquid
- 2 tablespoons of baking soda
- Vinegar

Let's Observe!

When you mix baking soda and vinegar together it makes bubbles. This is a chemical reaction!

What to do:

1. Mix salt, flour, oil, and water until smooth and firm.

2. Mold the dough around the plastic bottle and place the bottle on a plate. Be sure you don't cover the bottle's mouth.

3. Fill the bottle with warm water almost to the top. Add a few drops of food coloring.

4. Squeeze six drops of liquid detergent into the bottle. Add baking soda. Slowly pour some vinegar into the bottle. Make a prediction.

5. Was your prediction correct? What did you observe?

Murray's Science Words on the Street

fragment
A small piece that broke off of something bigger.

crust
A hard layer over something soft.

Super Sand

Quicksand is a very special kind of sand found near beaches, lakes, rivers, and swamps. It is made of sand mixed with water. The **viscosity** of quicksand depends on how much **pressure** or weight you put on it. If you were to fall into quicksand it would be very hard to get out. Why? Quicksand acts like a liquid when you move around in it slowly, and like a solid when you move around in it quickly. Amazing! Prairie Dawn and I are making our own quicksand out of cornstarch and water. But we are making our quicksand in a bowl so we do not have to worry about falling in!

What you need:
- A mixing bowl
- ¼ cup of cornstarch
- 1 cup of water

This isn't so super.

What to do:

1. Pour the cornstarch and water into the bowl and mix with your hands until it feels as thick as honey and looks like heavy cream.

2. Gently lay your hand on the surface and notice how your hand sinks into the mixture.

3. Now try to move your hand through it quickly. Feel how difficult it is to move. This is how real quicksand feels!

viscosity
The state of a being thick, sticky, and like a fluid.

pressure
Continuous force on or against something.

Murray's Science
Words on the Street

Itsy Bitsy Spider

Spiders and insects (bugs) are delight-fully creepy crawly, but did you know they are not the same thing? You can tell a spider (also called an arachnid) from an insect by counting the number of legs they have. Insects have six legs and spiders have eight. Twiddlebugs have two legs.

Circle all the spiders. How many are there all together? Now, count the insects. How many are there! How many Twiddlebugs do you see? Record your answers at the bottom of the page.

Insects _____   **Spiders** _____   **Twiddlebugs** _____

Here are some important spider numbers:

• There are many, many different kinds of spiders; 37,000 known species.

• Spiders spin webs out of silk, which shoots from 6 "spinnerets" on their bellies.

• Spiders have up to 12 eyes.

• They can lay up to 1,000 eggs at the same time. That's a lot of eggs!

For The Birds

The study of birds (like me!) is called **ornithology**. Scientists who study birds are called **ornithologists**. They examine birds' bodies, color, feathers, habits, songs, and how we fly. Winter is a great time to invite my feathered friends to visit your backyard or windowsill because it is when food is **scarce**.

My Sesame Street pals and I are making birdfeeders to make sure the birds get enough to eat. You can do it, too! Then, when birds arrive, pay careful attention to how they look, what they do, and the songs they sing.

What you need:
- Long pieces of string
- Pinecones and corncobs
- A spoon
- Peanut butter and birdseed
- *Science Journal* pages
- Crayons

Let's Observe!

Did you know some birds cannot fly? That is right! Penguins, ostriches, and kiwis are just some of the birds that cannot take off!

What to do:

1. Tie the long strings to the pinecones and corncobs.

2. Using the spoon, spread peanut butter all over the pinecones and corncobs; roll them in birdseed.

3. Hang the pinecones and corncobs from nearby trees.

4. Draw pictures of the birds that come to the birdfeeders in your *Science Journal* or a notebook.

5. Count the birds you see. How many did you see? What do you observe? Are some bigger than others? What colors are they?

BIRD SEED

PEANUT BUTTER

Murray's Science Words on the Street

ornithology
The study of birds.

ornithologist
A person who studies birds.

scarce
Few, rare.

More Fun With Birds...

Another way to **attract** birds to your yard is with a splish-splash birdbath. Birds drink water and also use it to clean their feathers. My friends and I are going to **engineer** our own birdbath, and then see which birds show up for bath time! Follow the instructions below and build your own birdbath. Birds on the go will love having a place to drink, bathe, and rest.

What you need:

- Crayons
- Pages from your *Science Journal* or notebook
- Weatherproof paint
- Paint brushes
- A plant pot
- Saucer (preferably an old one)
- Rocks
- Water
- Plastic gallon jug
- Strong string

I, Super Grover 2.0, can swoop, soar, and fly through the sky. Yet even a superhero like me cannot keep up with the peregrine falcon. This amazing bird flies way up high then dives down—whoosh! It is the fastest bird on earth.

What to do:

1. Using crayons, draw a picture or pattern in your *Science Journal* or notebook that you will want to paint on your pot.

2. Using the weatherproof paint and brushes, copy your picture or pattern onto the side of the pot. (You will be turning the pot upside down, so adjust the design, if necessary!)

3. Turn the plant pot over, then place the saucer on top of it. Set it under a tree. Place rocks in the saucer and fill it with water. (Rocks make it stable and give the birds a place to rest.)

4. To engineer the water jugs for the birdbath, ask a grown up to cut off the top of the plastic gallon jug and poke a tiny hole in the bottom. Tie strong string to the jug's handle, fill the jug with water, and hang it from a tree above the saucer so it will drip. Replace the water often to keep it clean. Fill the jug when it is empty.

Murray's Science Words on the Street

attract

To bring toward.

engineer

To design or build something for a certain purpose or to solve a problem.

75

Frankly, It's Becoming a Habitat

Birds live all over planet Earth. Seagulls fly near the ocean, and eagles soar above mountains. Penguins waddle on icebergs at the South Pole, and parrots perch on palms in the jungle. Any creature's home is called its **habitat.** My habitat is right here on Sesame Street! Draw a line to connect each bird to its habitat.

Mountains

Jungle

Ocean

Forest

South Pole

Sesame Street

Golden Eagle

Owl

Penguin

Parrot

Seagull

Big Bird

Murray's Science Word on the Street

habitat

A place where animals live and can find food, water, and a place to sleep.

Windsock It To Me

Elmo's fur feels all tickly when the wind blows. But when the wind is very strong, Elmo has to hold on tight just to stand up. Some people—like sailors and airplane pilots, need to know how windy it is outside before they go to work. A windsock is a great way to see the **force** and **direction** of the wind. When a windsock **droops,** it means the wind is barely blowing. But when a windsock flies **horizontally,** it means the wind is moving very fast.

Elmo and Rosita are making our own windsocks, and we will observe our windsocks to see if the wind is blowing fast or slow. Make your own windsock and learn more about the wind.

Es muy ventoso! That means "It's very windy" in Spanish!

What you need:

- An empty half-gallon ice cream tub and duct tape
- Sharp scissors
- Various craft supplies: Markers, stickers, construction paper, poster paint, glitter—whatever you like
- Crepe paper
- Strong tape
- 5 long pieces of string or yarn
- Pages from your *Science Journal*
- Crayons

What to do:

Make Your Windsock

1. Ask an adult to cut the bottom out of a tub (with lid removed) and duct tape all edges.

2. Decorate the outside of the tub.

3. Cut 6-10 strips of crepe paper, 2-feet long each; tape them to the bottom of the tub along the inside.

4. Punch 4 evenly spaced holes at the top edge of the tub. Thread 4 long pieces of string through the holes and knot together. Tie another long string through the knot to hang the windsock.

Observe Wind Speed and Direction

1. Look at the windsock and observe which way it is blowing. Is it hanging loose? Is it flying horizontal? Over the next few days, record what you have observed in your *Science Journal* or notebook.

2. Draw pictures of the weather you observe while you are studying your windsock. Is it rainy and windy? Sunny and calm? How do you think the weather and the wind are related?

force	**direction**	**droop**	**horizontal**
Strength or power.	The path in which something moves to or from something else.	To hang down in a limp way.	Lying in a flat line.

Murray's Science
Words on the Street

Free Fall

As a superhero, I **defy gravity** every day. What is gravity, you ask? It is a force that pulls everything toward the center of the earth. It is what makes you come down when you jump up; it is what stops water from flying out of the bathtub. I have always wondered if gravity would make something heavy—like a book—fall faster than something light—like a pencil.

My friends and I learned that all things fall at the same **rate,** no matter how much they weigh. But shape will affect the speed at which something falls. If an object catches air it will not drop as fast. That is why feathers and paper float to the ground. Collect a few objects and try it yourself. Use the power of observation to find out what happens!

What you need:

- 6 household items—some light, some heavy: A book, a Ping-Pong ball, a toy car, a pencil, a toy block, a feather, tissue paper, etc.
- A friend and/or a full-length mirror
- Pages from your *Science Journal* or notebook
- Crayons

What to do:

1. Put your 6 items in pairs, (i.e. a toy car and a book; a Ping-Pong ball and a block), side by side on a table.

2. Stand in front of a full-length mirror or ask a friend to watch as you drop two objects at the same time.

3. Observe what happened. Did the objects drop at the same rate? Did one drop faster or slower than the other? Was there something about the shape of the object that made a difference?

4. Mix up your objects and drop different pairs. Did anything different happen? Now try dropping the objects from a higher or lower point and see what happens.

5. Draw pictures of your objects and put check marks next to the things that fell quickly, and stars next to the ones that fell slowly.

defy

To go against rules, seem impossible.

gravity

An invisible force that pulls things toward the ground.

rate

Speed.

Murray's Science
Words on the Street

Come On and Compost

Hey, what's the big idea? Everyone used to throw their eggshells, banana peels and stuff they raked off their lawns into my trashcan. Now they're using all that awesome garbage for **composting**. Sure, compost is made from **decaying** material that has all kinds of **nutrients** in it to help plants grow strong and healthy.

But I miss all that extra garbage around here.

Still, composting is a form of recycling, and helps the earth. Elmo and Zoe are making an indoor composting container. Try it yourself. But save some garbage for me!

What you need:

- Plastic bottle and duct tape
- Scrap of mesh fabric like pantyhose, and a rubber band
- Plastic tub
- Scissors, spoon, or stick
- Browns—dead leaves, branches, twigs, etc; and Greens—eggshells, apple cores, carrot tops, coffee grounds, banana peels, etc.
- Dirt; shredded paper, such as cardboard toilet paper and paper towel rolls, and newspaper.
- Water

Supercharge your compost by adding worms like Slimey to the mixture (best for an outdoor compost.) Worms are nature's spoons. They tunnel through rotting material, mix it with their slime, (which is full of nutrients), and bring the material deep into the soil where it nourishes plant roots.

What to do:

1. Ask an adult to cut off the bottom ¼ of a plastic bottle and duct tape all edges. The bottom is your lid.

2. Place the scrap of mesh fabric over the spout and secure it with a rubber band.

3. Place the bottle upside down in the plastic tub. Have a grown up help you chop up the browns and greens then layer them into the bottle with dirt and shredded paper. (Don't use meat, dairy, bones, fats or oils.)

4. Add water and stir until everything is damp. Add the lid. Using a spoon or stick, stir a few times a week. Reuse any water that collects in the tub.

5. In a few weeks, check if your compost is ready. It should be dark and the materials you used should be unrecognizable. Add to the soil of houseplants or in your garden and watch the plants grow!

Murray's Science Words on the Street

compost
Rotting natural material used as plant fertilizer.

decay
To rot and fall apart.

nutrient
Food or something that helps living things grow healthy and strong.

Day In, Day Out

From where we stand on Earth, it seems like the sun moves around us. But really it is the Earth that is moving! Our planet **rotates** once every day and so the sun moves in and out of view. The thing is, our planet is so gigantic and moves so slowly that it is hard for us to see or feel it move.

That is why I have asked Abby and Cookie to help me pretend a rubber ball is the Earth and a flashlight is the sun. This will help us understand that the sun stays in one place while our planet (and we) move. It is really fun and easy, so go ahead and take your mini-Earth for a spin!

What you need:

- A crayon
- A rubber ball to represent the Earth
- A flashlight to represent the sun (a small, pen-sized flashlight is best)

Let's Observe!

I love to observe all the amazing colors at sunset. My favorite color is blue—like my fur!

What to do:

1. Using your crayon, draw a circle around the ball.

2. Draw an "X" anywhere along the circle. This marks where you are standing!

3. Shine the flashlight right at the "X"

4. Slowly turn the ball, making sure to keep the flashlight pointed at the line you have drawn. Watch as the "X" (you) move in and out of the light.

5. What do you observe? Is the whole ball lit up or is there a dark side? Which side of your mini-Earth do you think is in "daylight?" On which side is it "night?" Is there a line where the darkness starts and the light ends? Which of these lines do you think would be sunrise on the Earth? Which one would be the sunset?

rotate

To move in a circle around an imaginary center line.

Murray's Science Word on the Street

Answer Key

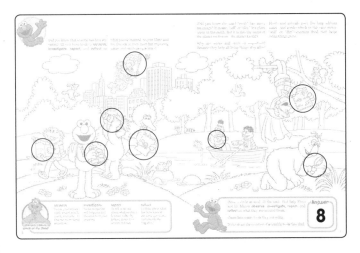

pages 6-7, Happy Scientists

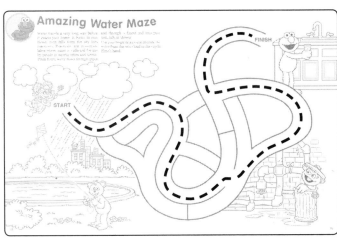

pages 18-19, Amazing Water Maze

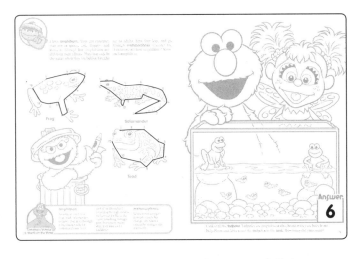

pages 28-29, Find the Amphibian

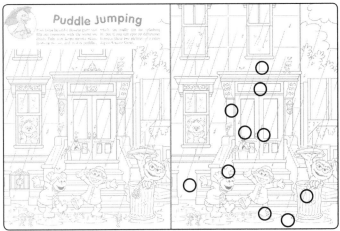

pages 38-39, Puddle Jumping

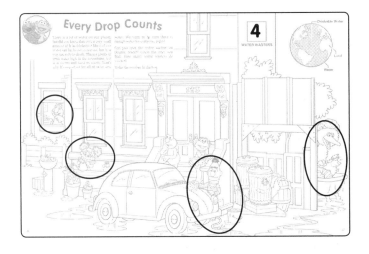

pages 46-47, Every Drop Counts

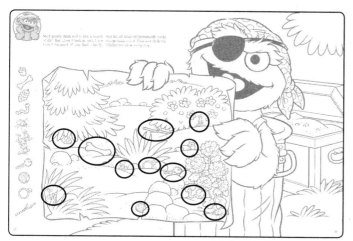

pages 58-59, Buried Treasure

Counting Tree Rings

4

3

6

5

pages 64-65, Counting Tree Rings

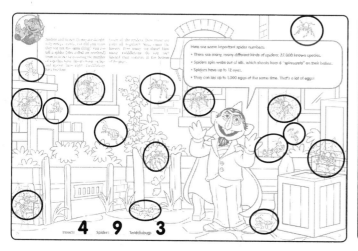

4   9   3

70-71, Itsy Bitsy Spider pages

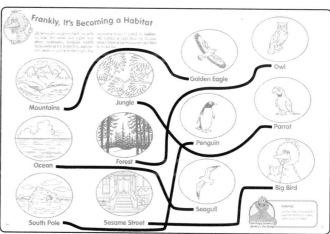

pages 76-77, Frankly, It's Becoming a Habitat

Science Journal

Observations

Science Journal

Observations

Science Journal

Observations

Science Journal

Observations

Science Journal

Observations

_____

_____

_____

_____

_____

_____

_____

_____

_____

Science Journal

Observations

Science Journal

Observations

Science Journal

Observations

Science Journal

Observations